# Decodable Stories

## Grade 3
## Book 3

*Bothell, WA • Chicago, IL • Columbus, OH • New York, NY*

MHEonline.com

Copyright © 2015 McGraw-Hill Education

All rights reserved. No part of this publication may be reproduced or distributed in any form or by any means, or stored in a database or retrieval system, without the prior written consent of McGraw-Hill Education, including, but not limited to, network storage or transmission, or broadcast for distance learning.

Send all inquiries to:
McGraw-Hill Education
8787 Orion Place
Columbus, OH 43240

ISBN: 978-0-07-671887-0
MHID: 0-07-671887-5

Printed in the United States of America.

2 3 4 5 6 7 8 9 DOC 20 19 18 17 16 15

# Table of Contents

12  The Empty Field. . . . . . . . . . . . . . . . . . . . . . . . 1
13  Bats. . . . . . . . . . . . . . . . . . . . . . . . . . . . . . . . . 9
14  More Bats . . . . . . . . . . . . . . . . . . . . . . . . . . 17
15  Condors . . . . . . . . . . . . . . . . . . . . . . . . . . . 25
16  A Visit . . . . . . . . . . . . . . . . . . . . . . . . . . . . . 33
17  Migrating Geese . . . . . . . . . . . . . . . . . . . . 41

Decodable Stories' Table . . . . . . . . . . . . . . . . . 49

# The Empty Field

by Daniel Fairwood
illustrated by Luanne Martin

**Decodable Story 12**

Bothell, WA • Chicago, IL • Columbus, OH • New York, NY

This may look like it is only an empty field. But it is not. There is a lot of life concealed in this field. It is an important habitat for many plants and animals. Let's go see what we can find.

Can you see this baby deer sleeping in the green grass? His spots help hide him from being seen. He seems at ease, but he knows he must stay ready. He listens closely, and studies each crunch or splash he hears. Is that a nearby stream or an enemy closing in?

It's a wild turkey and her family! The series of chirps and cheeps is coming from her babies. They are not a danger to the deer. The turkeys are only looking for seeds, leaves, and berries to eat. They ignore the baby deer and keep looking for any hidden treats.

Buzzing above the turkey family is a bee. The bee is also looking for something to eat. He spots a large daisy and buzzes close. He will collect pollen and take it back to the queen bee. She is a part of a hive near the edge of the field.

The beehive is in a tree on the border of the field. The bees made their hive in the trunk of a beech tree. The bees return to the hive with pollen for the queen. Other bees buzz nearby.

Dug in beneath the beech tree is a bunny rabbit. Bunnies can hear very well because they have large ears. The bunny can hear the bees buzzing above. But she knows the bees do not want to hurt her.

She also hears an eagle screeching in the air above. He is looking for a tasty snack. The eagle has sharp eyes, but the bunny is hidden. That means the field looks empty to the eagle too, and he glides away to look for something to eat in a different field.

# Bats

by Curtis Brinkman
illustrated by Meryl Henderson

**Decodable Story 13**

Bothell, WA • Chicago, IL • Columbus, OH • New York, NY

Bats! These strange flying animals frighten some kids and amaze others. One thing is apparent. Not many kids think bats are boring!

Yet, there are things kids do not understand about bats. And some things that kids think about bats are just wrong.

Here are bat facts that you might like to know and share.

**Bats are not birds.**

Bats fly, so they must be birds. Right? Wrong! Bats are mammals.
- Birds have feathers. Mammals have fur or hair.
- Mammals are born live. Birds hatch from eggs.
- Mammals give milk to their babies. Birds do not.

And birds can fly, but mammals cannot—except for bats! That's why bats are amazing.

**Bats are not rodents.**
    Some kids think of bats as flying rats or mice. Rats and mice are rodents. Rodents are little mammals with strong teeth. Squirrels, beavers, and gophers are rodents, too, but bats are not.
    Here is a surprise: Bats are more like apes and chimps than rodents!

**Bats are not blind.**
    You may have heard the phrase, "as blind as a bat." Yet bats are not blind. Bats see well. But bats also send invisible waves as they fly. These waves reflect off things. These waves help bats find and catch insects at night. For bats, these waves are even better than sight!

**Bats hide well.**

Do bats live near you? Bats might, but it is hard to tell. Bats sleep out of sight in daytime. Bats fly and hunt for bugs at night.

Where can bats sleep? Bats can doze in barns, caves, high up in trees, or under bridges. And bats don't lie down to sleep. Bats sleep hanging upside down.

**Bats help people and habitats.**

People need bats. Why? Bats eat lots of bugs. Some bugs harm farmers' crops.

Bats live in most habitats. And bats help each habitat that they live in. In some places, bats are like bees. Bats help plants survive.

And bats can help you. How? The next story will tell more.

# More Bats

by Ella Cherup
illustrated by Meryl Henderson

**Decodable Story 14**

A gentle wind was blowing. "The breeze feels nice," said Cody.

"Yes," agreed Joan. "A breeze after a slow, long rain is refreshing."

Cody and Joan looked at a meadow next to Joan's house. There were little puddles of water here and there. "But those puddles frighten me a bit," Cody admitted.

"Puddles frighten you? Why?" asked Joan.

"Puddles are places for bugs," said Cody. "Insects lay lots of eggs in puddles. Then more bugs hatch and grow. And the bugs are bad ones. They bite people!"

"I know about bugs and puddles," said Joan. "But the same puddles do not frighten me."

"Why not?" asked Cody.

"I will show you," replied Joan.

Joan led Cody to the side of her house. She showed him an odd-looking box. It was on a pole next to an oak tree. "Do you know what this is?"

"No," said Cody.

"It is a bat box," explained Joan.

"A *bat* box!" said a surprised Cody.

"Yes, it is made from cedar lumber," said Joan. "Bats like cedar."

"Bats!" said Cody. The term stuck in his throat. "You mean those creepy little things with wings?"

Joan smiled. "Yes," she said.

"I know why people have bird houses," said Cody. "But why would you have a bat box?"

"My dad made it," Joan said. "He hung it so bats might live here."

Cody was shocked. "Did it work?" he asked.

"Yes," said Joan. "An entire bat colony lives in the box."

"That means loads of bats! Why?" asked Cody. He looked a little afraid. He slowly backed away from the pole.

"Well, do you know what bats eat?" asked Joan.

"No," said Cody.

"Bugs!" smiled Joan. "A bat eats 500 bugs in a short time. A bat colony eats bugs all night."

"Your bats protect you from meadow puddles!" Cody said.

"Yes," said Joan. "Our bats will eat those bugs."

Cody said, "That means I can like bats."

Joan smiled. "Unless you are a bug!" she said.

# Condors

by Ella Cherup
illustrated by Meryl Henderson

**Decodable Story 15**

This story tells about another animal that helps humans. Without human help, this huge bird would not have survived.

Some people argue that a condor is an ugly-looking bird. Why? It has fluffy feathers all over its body. But its head looks like it has been shaved. That makes a condor's head seem too small. Plus the condor's face is often pink, red, or blue. In the middle of that face is a huge, odd-looking beak.

Yet when a condor flies, people change their minds about its looks. It is the biggest bird in the United States. Its wings stretch nine to ten feet apart. The undersides of its wings are white, outlined by black.

Up in the air, a condor is an incredible sight. It often seems to fly without working at it. It just seems to float.

Long ago, people called the condor by another name. They called it the thunderbird. The condor seemed so big that when it flapped its wings, it could make thunder! Few can deny how amazing the thunderbird looks flying high up in the sky. People continue to think that the condor stands for strength.

In its habitat, a condor has real value. A condor does not kill animals to survive. It eats animals that have died! That seems yucky, but it's good. Condors help keep our world clean.

And each condor can help the world for a long time. Some condors live sixty years.

Yet for a while, not many condors had a chance to live that long. We humans hurt their habitat. We hurt condors. Condors came close to dying out. In the 1980s, just a few of these large birds were left.

Humans harmed condors, but humans also helped them. In the 1980s, a plan was started to rescue condors.

That rescue plan continues. Now, in cliffs high in the air, male and female condors sit on eggs and wait for condor babies to hatch. We wait, too. We want condors around for a long time.

# A Visit

by Ella Cherup
illustrated by Meryl Henderson

**Decodable Story 16**

Bothell, WA • Chicago, IL • Columbus, OH • New York, NY

Pretend we are visiting an Arizona desert habitat. Truly, the best time to go is on a spring morning. Summer is too hot. Spring is much cooler.

We should expect to see lots of sand in a desert. And we do! But the desert is also filled with amazing plants. In springtime, many plants bloom.

The biggest plant is the cactus. Our eyes zoom to a large one. It looms fifty feet up in the blue sky. It has blooms on it. These are creamy white with yellow centers. As this day grows hot, the blooms will close. By late June, they will not be around.

And look! Morning dew sits on the cactus.

The cactus is not smooth. It has two-inch-long spikes all over. They are called *spines*. Spines keep the cactus cool. They protect it from some animals, too.

A cactus does not need much rain. Its roots do not extend too far. But the roots soak up water when it rains. The cactus swells to store that water.

Do you see those holes in the cactus? Birds flew here and made those. Animals use the cactus for food. Due to the fact that a cactus stores water, animals use it to get water, too.

Holes can harm a cactus. Fluid can ooze out. But a cactus can reduce that harm by sealing those holes closed.

Bees and bats drink nectar from cactus blooms. This helps the cactus. Bees and bats carry bits of pollen from one bloom to another. Pollen helps cactus seeds grow. Those seeds drop to the desert. Soon new cacti grow!

A cactus can live a long time. A few may live as long as 200 years. That's the truth!

We should end our visit. Too bad we cannot stay. At night, a cactus is like a zoo. Animals, birds, and bugs visit it for food and drink. At night, we would see proof of how much desert life needs cacti.

Next, read about kids who have fun using what they know about an animal and its habitat.

# Migrating Geese

by Tony Parker
illustrated by Lynne Avril

**Decodable Story 17**

Bothell, WA • Chicago, IL • Columbus, OH • New York, NY

Little Eva began flapping her arms slowly and smoothly. Sue watched her and grinned. "Eva, what are you pretending to be?" she asked.

"I am a goose," said Eva. "I am a goose on the loose!"

"I knew it!" said Sue. She began to flap her arms, too. "I am up in the blue sky, too."

Eva and Sue ran slowly around the yard. They passed the wading pool. Eva nodded to it.

"Do you see the pond below us?" yelled Eva.

Sue pretended the pool was a pond. "Yes," she yelled back.

"We just flew from there. It is our summer habitat in a valley. But now we are flying away," Eva told Sue.

"I know why," said Sue. "The weather is turning cool. Soon the pond will freeze!"

Eva ran fast and zoomed around Sue. She continued flapping her arms. "You are right, Goose Sue," she said. "We are migrating to our winter home."

"How many geese are following us?" asked Sue.

"Quite a few," explained Eva.

The girls ran a bit more. "I am the goose leader!" said Eva. "I rule!"

Sue smiled at her little sister. "Okay. I am following you!"

"We are flying over vast open fields," added Eva. "Let's swoop down for a closer look."

Both girls turned and dipped on one side. Eva led Sue through the garden sprinkler.

"We are flying through a strong storm," yelled Eva.

Both girls pretended the storm blew them up and down as they approached it.

Then the girls flew along the sandbox. "See that patch below. It's a desert," yelled Eva.

"Do geese fly over deserts?" asked Sue.

"The truth is that I do not know," said Eva.

The sisters flew past Dad. He smiled. What were they doing? Their flapping arms were a clue. Dad played along. He cried to the girls, "Excuse me, little goofy ducks, but it is noon. It's time for lunch."

Eva stopped flapping. "Dad! We are not goofy ducks. We are goofy geese!" she said.

Sue chuckled. "That is true!"

Dad and Eva chuckled, too.

# Decodable Stories' Table

## Getting Started

| Lesson | Core Decodable | Practice Decodable | Sound/Spelling Correspondences | High-Frequency Words Introduced |
|---|---|---|---|---|
| Day 1 | 1 Matt, Kim, and Sam | 1 Sam | /a/ spelled *a*<br>/d/ spelled *d*<br>/h/ spelled *h_*<br>/m/ spelled *m*<br>/n/ spelled *n*<br>/s/ spelled *s, ss*<br>/t/ spelled *t, tt*<br>/i/ spelled *i*<br>/o/ spelled *o*<br>/b/ spelled *b*<br>/k/ spelled *c, k*<br>/f/ spelled *f, ff*<br>/g/ spelled *g* | hand, high, land, watch |
| Day 2 | 2 Fast Sam | 2 Help | /e/ spelled *e, _ea_*<br>/j/ spelled *j*<br>/l/ spelled *l, ll*<br>/p/ spelled *p*<br>/r/ spelled *r*<br>/ks/ spelled ■*x*<br>/u/ spelled *u*<br>/kw/ spelled *qu_*<br>/v/ spelled *v*<br>/w/ spelled *w_*<br>/y/ spelled *y_*<br>/z/ spelled *z, zz, _s* | hear, next, still, until |
| Day 3 | 3 Midge | 3 Fran and Ann | /j/ spelled ■*dge*<br>/k/ spelled ■*ck*<br>/ng/ spelled ■*ng*<br>/nk/ spelled ■*nk*<br>/a/ spelled *a*<br>/e/ spelled *e, _ea_*<br>/i/ spelled *i*<br>/o/ spelled *o*<br>/u/ spelled *u* | back, children, head, move, plants, second |
| Day 4 | 4 Tell Your Pals | 4 Fran's Story | /ar/ spelled *ar*<br>/er/ spelled *er, ir, ur, ear*<br>/or/ spelled *or, ore* | earth, hard, last, more, school, story, than |
| Day 5 | 5 Stars | 5 Fishing | /sh/ spelled *sh*<br>/th/ spelled *th*<br>/ch/ spelled *ch* | above, answer, friend, night, turned |

## Unit 1

| Lesson | Core Decodable | Practice Decodable | Sound/Spelling Correspondences | High-Frequency Words Introduced |
|---|---|---|---|---|
| Lesson 1 | 6 Val's New Bike | 6 Dave's New Home | /ā/ spelled *a, a_e*<br>/ī/ spelled *i, i_e*<br>/ō/ spelled *o, o_e* | change, find, home, most, talk, thought |
| Lesson 2 | 7 Vic's Big Chore | 7 Dave Returns | /ē/ spelled *e, e_e*<br>/ū/ spelled *u, u_e* | close, time, while |
| Lesson 3 | 8 Gem Is Missing | 8 More Clover | /j/ spelled *ge, gi_*<br>/s/ spelled *ce, ci_, cy* | large, name, things |
| Lesson 4 | 9 On a Train | 9 Riddles | /ā/ spelled *ai_, _ay*<br>/ə/ spelled *_le, _el, _al, _il* | city, each, face, near, through, took |
| Lesson 5 | 10 Bike Races | 10 Dad Wraps a Gift | /f/ spelled *ph*<br>/m/ spelled *_mb*<br>/n/ spelled *kn_*<br>/r/ spelled *wr_*<br>/w/ spelled *wh_* | almost, also, years |
| Lesson 6 | 11 Too Cold? | 11 I Was Inside a Dragon | Review Lessons 1–5 | air, such |

## Unit 2

| Lesson | Core Decodable | Practice Decodable | Sound/Spelling Correspondences | High-Frequency Words Introduced |
|---|---|---|---|---|
| Lesson 1 | 12 The Empty Field | 12 Lee's Eagle | /ē/ spelled *ee, ea, _y, _ie_, _ey* | eyes, part |
| Lesson 2 | 13 Bats | 13 Mack's Problem | /ī/ spelled *_igh, _ie, _y* | even, might, need, trees |
| Lesson 3 | 14 More Bats | 14 An Old Boat | /ō/ spelled *oa_, _ow* | house, same, side |
| Lesson 4 | 15 Condors | 15 Mew? Mew? | /ū/ spelled *_ew, _ue* | feet, world, without |
| Lesson 5 | 16 A Visit | 16 Yikes! Sue! | /o͞o/ spelled *oo, u, u_e, _ew, _ue* | end, should |
| Lesson 6 | 17 Migrating Geese | 17 Strange Stuff | Review Lessons 1–5 | along, began, following |

## Grade 3 High-Frequency Words

| | | | | |
|---|---|---|---|---|
| above | earth | high | night | than |
| air | end | home | paper | things |
| almost | enough | house | part | thought |
| along | even | land | plants | through |
| also | ever | large | point | time |
| answer | eyes | last | same | took |
| back | face | letters | school | trees |
| began | feet | might | second | turned |
| between | find | more | set | until |
| book | following | most | should | watch |
| change | friend | move | side | while |
| children | hand | name | still | without |
| city | hard | near | story | words |
| close | head | need | such | world |
| each | hear | next | talk | years |

## Grade 2 High-Frequency Words

| | | | | |
|---|---|---|---|---|
| again | easy | many | people | these |
| always | eight | may | picture | think |
| animal | everyone | mouse | piece | those |
| another | everything | Mr. | please | three |
| because | far | Mrs. | pull | today |
| been | few | much | quite | together |
| believe | first | myself | read | uncle |
| better | full | never | seven | under |
| black | give | new | show | upon |
| both | goes | nine | sign | us |
| bring | gray | off | small | use |
| brother | great | often | something | warm |
| brought | hold | once | soon | wash |
| buy | horse | only | sorry | which |
| carry | knew | open | start | white |
| center | laugh | other | stop | who |
| circle | learn | ought | taste | why |
| different | light | our | tell | work |
| does | listen | own | ten | write |
| done | live | paste | thank | zero |

## Grade 1 High-Frequency Words

| | | | | |
|---|---|---|---|---|
| about | come | how | one | too |
| after | could | if | or | two |
| an | day | into | over | very |
| any | don't | its | pretty | walk |
| are | every | jump | put | want |
| around | five | just | red | water |
| ask | four | know | ride | way |
| away | from | like | right | well |
| before | get | long | saw | went |
| big | going | make | six | where |
| blue | good | me | sleep | will |
| brown | got | my | take | would |
| by | green | no | their | yellow |
| call | help | now | them | yes |
| came | here | old | this | your |

## Grade K High-Frequency Words

| | | | | |
|---|---|---|---|---|
| a | did | her | on | they |
| all | do | him | out | to |
| am | down | his | said | up |
| and | for | I | see | was |
| as | girl | in | she | we |
| at | go | is | some | were |
| be | had | it | that | what |
| boy | has | little | the | when |
| but | have | look | then | with |
| can | he | of | there | you |

52